A PERFECT GUIDE TO PLANNING
Bar / Bat / B'nai Mitzvah

First Edition

Robert A. Starkey

INDEX

+ 4 BONUS OFFERS!

Organization

The key to pulling off a successful Bar Mitzvah or Bat Mitzvah is to be organized from the get-go. Create a timeline of what needs to be done by when. Mark reminders on your calendar. Do whatever is necessary to keep your planning orderly. Even if you fail to start planning as early as you could, if you maintain organization, you can pull of a successful Bar/Bat Mitzvah in a shorter amount of time. Just remember to make a schedule and stick to it.

You can start planning as early as 2 years in advance. Use this time to set a date from the Temple/Synagogue. You can also set a budget and determine the type of Simcha event that you would like - daytime or evening and the level of formality. Create a preliminary guest list because you'll need an estimate of the number of guests. This will be required to book your reception hall and/or caterer. You can also book your photographer and videographer. Booking the necessities this early will give you plenty of choice. You will be able to have a selection and choose the best for your particular event based upon a combination of quality and price.

At a year and a half you can book your DJ or musicians for the event. You might also look into less traditional forms of entertainment. You could hire a magician or caricaturist. You could have virtual reality games set up. Be creative. What would your child and the guests enjoy? At this point you can also finalize a color scheme as well as a theme for the party if applicable.

Six to 12 months before the Mitzvah, your child will no doubt have started learning his or her portion of the Torah. Investigate florists and settle upon one for the Synagogue service as well as for the Kiddush table and other table centerpieces. Determine the design of any balloon displays that you will have. You may also need to book a hotel for your out of town guests. At this point you should also begin shopping for Bar/Bat Mitzvah clothing.

As you get closer you will need to finalize your guest list, order invitations, and order any other items. You will need to create a song list, have photos taken, and pay all of your fees. The key to pulling off such an important and intricate event is this organization. Make a list of everything that needs to be done before the day of the event. Write down every detail. Then you can categorize your list by importance and what needs to be done in what order. Your child has his or her own responsibilities in preparing for the ceremony, so the bulk of the planning will fall to you the parent. You will need to make decisions about entertainment forms and decorations. Try to involve your child, but the major decision making will be yours. There will be problems and hitches, but if you stay on track and organized, you will be better prepared to handle the little upsets which come along the way.

Schedules

As you've probably already discovered, schedules are the core of what holds your event planning on track for the big day. You need to write due dates, deadlines, and appointments into a calendar or schedule format to keep on top of everything. A schedule for the Bar/Bat Mitzvah itself is also required. People need to know what is going on when and where.

Without an itinerary, you should prepare yourself for absolute chaos. It is so bad that most venues, caterers, entertainers, and DJ's will require a schedule several weeks before that day. You'll need to create one and provide it to anyone who needs or requests it. This includes everyone working at the event plus any family or friends who may be assisting in the activities for the day. The number one important person to give a schedule to is your DJ. He or she needs to know when to direct people to food and other activities. He/she is your directing voice for the event and must be always informed.

So, how do you make a schedule? Simply create a time table. Start with the beginning of the ceremony. Make a chart describing what events will occur at which times.

For example:

Time- arrive at Temple w/ child
Time-photographer arrives
Time-ceremony begins
Time-DJ/band arrives at venue
Time-ceremony ends
Time-guests arrive at venue
Time-parents and child arrive at venue
Time-dinner is served

Fill in the blanks, and continue throughout the rest of the event until the guests will depart. Every activity should be written down and time slot specified. You may be unsure of specifics early on, but as time progresses and you draw closer to the date, you will be able to fill in the blanks. Draw up a rough itinerary as early as possible, so that at least you know what kind of goal you are aiming for.

Despite all of your careful planning, you can be assured that the course of events will not follow your schedule to perfection. Your itinerary cannot prevent traffic on the way to the hall, or fix a caterer's mistake. Things will go wrong, and activities will be delayed. Don't panic though; things are allowed to go wrong because you have your schedule to fall back on. Schedules are always subject to change on the day of the event. The schedule will, however, keep everything from falling apart when slight hitches do occur. You will have an easier time putting the event back on track if you have a track set out to follow. Otherwise you may forget some activities, and the occasion will fall apart with guests lost in confusion. People need to remain informed throughout the event. Your DJ should be aware of the itinerary and your desires. His/her responsibility will be to inform your guests of dinner time and other activities.

Make Check lists

Making a check lists can be a very helpful way of keeping track precisely of everything that needs to be done. You can make a list of things to do, things to buy, people to call, things to bring to the synagogue, things to bring to the party, people to honor, people to photograph, etc. This will make organizing your Bar Mitzvah much easier.

One of the best lists you can make is a list of people who need to be photographed. Prepare a list of photos you want to be taken and tables you want photographed. If you are hiring a photographer, you should make sure that he receives the list before the  event. It is a good idea to make two extra copies of the photography list. Assign these lists to two different people. One person to check off all the photographs that have already been taken and another to notify the people who will be in the next shot.

Making a list of things that need to be done, can help you organize particular things that need to be done on a particular day. This is a helpful way of ensuring everything is done on time. Write down all the things that need to be completed in the order in which you want to complete them. It is very important that you label all your lists, otherwise you can easily become confused. Write what every list is for, in black marker or pen, on top of each list.

Making a list of things that need to be bought will ensure that you buy all the things you require for this special day. Go through everything you will need and write the items down as they come to mind. If you have a limited budget you can arrange the items on your list from most important to least important. This will allow you to see which items can be cut from the list if you start to run low on money.

Create a list of people you need to call for example: the caterer. This will ensure that everything is organized and ready for the big day.

Make a list of people who need to be honored. This will ensure that you do not forget to mention anyone in a speech or when writing thank you notes. Read thorough the guest list thoroughly and write down the names of the people you wish to honor.

Make a list of things that need to be brought to the party or synagogue. One can tend to forget or leave things behind in the excitement of the big day.

Make copies of all your lists. When organizing a big event such as a Bar Mitzvah or Bat Mitzvah, lists have a tendency to disappear. Keeping copies of lists will prevent any extra stress and discomfort.

Manage your time. Make sure everything is done and that you will arrive at the venue on time. This will keep you relaxed and make the day more enjoyable.

Tips and Tricks for Business Dealings

During the planning of your child's Bar/Bat Mitzvah, you will have, as they say, a lot of irons in the fire. You have to be careful to not allow your enthusiasm for this occasion to cloud your business judgment. There are several do's and don'ts to keep in mind to protect yourself from being taken advantage of.

First of all, do require a written contract from any vendors which you employ for the event. And don't place any money down without a copy of this contract. He/she may try to convince you that it is not their standard protocol to fill out contracts at this point. Shady business people will often try to take advantage of people hosting onetime events. They will assume that you don't know what you're doing. Do be confident, and don't allow them to walk all over you. Regardless of how beautiful a photographer's examples are or how well recommended a DJ or band is, demand a signed contract before giving them one cent. Also, don't pay the full amount until the latest date possible before the event. You never know what could happen. Generally vendors require the full amount two weeks before. Others allow you to pay the day of the event if you pay cash.

Do hire those who are well recommended, but don't hire relatives. Relatives generally won't charge as much as others if at all, but you will have far less input into the results. Relatives will often take the event more casually because they are not being paid or because they are family. It's harder to enforce deadlines and appointment times with relatives who are doing you a favor. Some relatives may take the job professionally and do a great job of it. If they don't do their best, however, you risk poor quality plus you may jeopardize aspects of the relationship.

Do follow through with your expectations. If you have a contract, use it to your advantage. If a vendor tries to give you the run-around, simply remind him/her of their legal obligations. You need not burst out with a letter from your lawyer. An email or phone call describing your expectation and their necessary obligations will probably do the trick.

Simply say, "According to the contract I'm reading, you should be providing us with such and such, by this date, or a full refund will be granted. When can we expect you to follow through on this?"

Regardless of what happens, keep a cool, business minded head. Don't allow yourself to be carried away. Don't be talked into purchasing more services than you need. Make a game plan with what you want and how much you want to spend. Allow some room for unrealistic expectations, if no vender in the area will do it for that price. Don't be taken for a fool, however. Stay alert and be firm, and your business deals should proceed without a hitch, aiding greatly to your child's momentous day.

Budgeting Tips

The first key to maintaining a successful budget is to trim your guest list. With a smaller headcount, you can spring for better quality and more upscale items to create a once-in-a-lifetime experience for your child and your guests. Make it a day that nobody will forget. This is the quickest way to improve your bottom line. If you want an intimate affair, distant friends won't be upset that they were not invited. People understand that theses are expensive celebrations. Be sure also to balance the ratio of children to adults. You don't want a total kiddy party, but neither should the children be outnumbered by the grown-ups. You may not want that many children, but keep in mind that children's menus cost less than adults'. Also keep in mind that this is a celebration for your child, so he or she should have some say in who is invited.

Time and day is another key issue to consider. Saturday night may be the most obvious time to hold your event. This obvious solution comes with a price. Some vendors charge more to operate during this peak time. It may be just as convenient to have the celebration on another day and time. If it is just as easy, than you may be able to save a bundle by doing so. Also keep in mind that if you want to reserve something for the peak time, than you will need to reserve it early because these time slots fill up the fastest.

Another way to save a lot of money is to determine what you can do yourself. You don't want your event to look homemade. Everything should look professional, but some things may not require a paid professional's touch to look nice. There are plenty of tasks to complete that are easy enough for a parent or other family member to do. For example, you may be able to buy fabric and create beautiful tablecloths for half of the price that it would cost to buy them. Be sure to do your homework first though, because in some situations, it is more cost effective to give the job to a vendor.

Choose your location carefully. You may think immediately that having the reception at your home will save you a great deal of money. This is not necessarily the case. If you have the party at a house, you will be at least doubling the amount of items and services which you will need to rent. You will need a dance floor, lighting, place settings, and food. Some locations include everything that you will need. These are usually the best bargains.

Always keep in mind that you cannot necessarily have everything how you would like it within a rigid budget. Choose your priorities, that is, focus on the items of most importance to you. If you are excited about a particular band to have at the event, but don't care so much about the food, than spend accordingly. Go a little higher on your music budget, but be more frugal with your food spending. Have a few elements that wow people, and the rest can be more normal. Your celebration can still be nothing short of fantastic, even while on a budget.

Low Budget Events

So your child's Bar/Bat Mitzvah could not come at a worse time financially speaking. You've recently sank buckets of money into repairs for the car, and family health problems are also draining the bank. Whatever your situation is, you don't have spare money to throw an amazing celebration for your child. You feel bad because you know that he/she deserves the best. Don't despair; you can still hold an unforgettable event even on the tightest of budgets.

If you have some money to spare, but not much, you'll need to pick what's important. You can't have catered food, plus a DJ, plus a magician. You'll need to determine what means the most to you and to your child. What would you miss the most if it wasn't there? You might also consider shrinking your guest list in order to expand what you will be able to provide for them at the event- a quality over quantity idea. However, this is up to you, as you do not want to offend close friends.

As far as venues go, your best bet will be to hold the event at someone's house. Whoever has the most spacious home in your family could probably be swayed into hosting the reception. If you are imposing on a relative like this, than make sure that this is all that this person is being asked to do. You take care of all of the decorations in the home, and everything else that is involved. House events can be just as fun and elegant as banquet halls.

Now obviously if you try to cram 200 people into a 2,000 square foot home, it's not going to work out. So you will need to adjust your guest list based upon the size of the chosen home. Especially if it is not your own home, you do not want personal property to be damaged. If the home has a pool, you could even theme it as a pool party. Have the kids bring swim suits and pool toys

If the event is small scale, the family can prepare a meal for the guests. If you are hosting more than 50 or so people, however, this probably won't work. Even over 20 would be a stretch. Instead have a pot luck dinner. If you theme the dinner and have people bring ethnic foods, it will not seem tacky. Guests will be excited to try their hand at cooking different types of dishes. At any rate, nobody will say anything, even if they do disapprove. And if they don't like it, they probably shouldn't have been on the final guest list anyways.

Regardless of how small the gathering is, the event will be wonderful and memorable because of the significance of your child's important day. You will make memories, and even if they are displayed on disposable camera prints, it won't change the smiles on everyone's faces. The point of the celebration is to bring together family and friends to joyfully celebrate your child's life and spiritual commitment. Lack of money takes nothing away from the real meaning.

Budget Cutting

So you've gotten a little carried away while planning your child's dream Bar/Bat Mitzvah. Did you get so excited that you ordered an over abundance of expensive roses? Or did you fail to restrain yourself in some other manner? You may have planned for an extravaganza, but another pressing expense came up. Whatever the case may be, it's not too late to fix your mistakes. You probably have deposits on everything, but the full amount is not due until much closer.

You can still fix things without it looking like you had to cut your budget.

People tend to allow flowers to get the best of them. The florist may put together a centerpiece packed with beauty, and part of you jumps out and says, "I'll take it!" without considering the price of such a full arrangement. Roses tend to cost more than other flowers. Also the less greenery you have, the more flowers you'll get in a fuller looking arrangement. More flowers and less green requires more green from you. Don't be afraid to go back to the florist and have him show you a scaled back version of your arrangement. Keep things a little looser and airier and it will still look elegant and expensive without costing you so much.

Food is an area in which it is hard to scale back too much. You can, however, if you do it properly and with a good caterer. A good caterer won't mind being asked to cook less expensive dishes for you. A not-so-good one may not do as good a job on less expensive food, especially if you are asking him to downgrade from a previous fancier selection. Definitely know who you're dealing with when selecting a caterer. A good money saving option is to provide two different menus- one for the kids and one for adults. The kids won't mind eating pizza, and this allows for the adults to enjoy a nicer meal.

There are plenty of options to lower your dress/attire budget. You don't want to limit your son or daughter by making them cut corners too much. For your own attire, there are many ways to save. Start shopping far in advance. This way you can be on the lookout for sales. You can also shop at discount / consignment shops to find good bargains. If you're in a hurry and waited until the last minute, you won't have as many choices. As long as you're not rushed you can find plenty of good deals on dresses that will make you look great without breaking the bank.

Keep in mind the reason for the event. You want to throw a fun celebration in honor of the milestone in your child's life. You don't, however want to put yourself into debt over it. As long as you have good family and friends gathered together to share in the occasion, that's all you need. The rest is just icing on the cake, so don't worry about impressing anybody.

Don't Get Carried Away

 There is often a strong tendency of the party or reception to overshadow the importance of the ceremony which precedes it. You don't want your child to get caught up in party/present mode and fail to realize the significance of this step in his or her life. This should be a time of celebration, but it should also be a time of reflection for both you and your child. Use the time wisely, and keep the party from taking over your family and spiritual lives. The time should be spent instead of thinking about the party, in thinking about each other. Treasure the time given to you to spend with your child, teaching him or her, and just appreciating him/her as another person. Don't let the party excitement rob you of the emotional and spiritual aspect of a Bar/Bat Mitzvah.

Try to keep your child focused upon the seriousness of the matter. Don't exclude him or her from party planning events. Simultaneously, don't allow him/her to skip studying the Torah in lieu of going to the party store. Talk to him or her seriously about why it is that you are going to celebrate with this party. Explain the tradition of Bar/Bat Mitzvahs and their spiritual significance. You can also use the opportunity to show your child his/her own personal family history. Talk about it but be careful not to lecture. If you slip into lecture mode, your child will immediately view the talk as punishment and he or she will stop paying attention, and they certainly won't care to learn any more or ask questions. Try to inspire questions within your child about the faith and traditions.

Another way to prevent the party from taking over your entire mentality and your child's is to make an effort to spend some time together. Have quality family time in the months leading up to the Bar/Bat Mitzvah. You may find that it is hard to schedule in time with all of the business, but this kind of hard to find time proves to be the most rewarding. You could go on a family camping trip one weekend. This will get you away from the hectic nature of planning, and you will get to spend time with your family building memories.

You will also want to spend some one-on-one time with your son or daughter before the big day. Don't use the time to harass them about their Torah studying, or lecture on Jewish traditions. Simply go to lunch and hang out with your child. Talk to them about topics important and interesting to them.   You never want to take for granted the time that you have with your child. So spend a day with him or her doing something that he/she would enjoy.

Prevent Stress

Planning any major event is stressful. Planning a Bar/Bat Mitzvah can be even more challenging for various reasons. First of all you need to take into account your child's opinion and desires for the occasion because it is his/her day after all. You are also planning a party that will be enjoyable to both children and adults; this in itself is a conundrum. This pressure to please everyone can lead to a great deal of stress for you as a planner and a parent. There are steps you can take, however, to prevent and relieve this stress during the course of your planning.

The easiest solution for any stressed out parent is to hire an event planner to do most of your leg work for you. Event planners are great because they have the experience necessary to deal with vendors appropriately. They also often have great creative tips to offer. So if you find yourself at a roadblock, you can consult your planner to figure out ideas for activities, food or whatever. The downside to event planners is that they can be expensive. In addition, you may feel as though they are not doing anything that you are not capable of doing yourself. The difference is that they get paid for their work, so they have more patience and time to spend contacting people and following up with vendors.

If you are going to plan this event yourself, be prepared. This is hard work, and sometimes it seems impossible to do within even the most flexible time constraints. Keep in mind that everything will work out. Things will eventually fall into place even if it gets messy in the middle. Everybody needs a break once in awhile. You won't be doing anyone any good if you are frazzled to the point of near insanity. Therefore, treat yourself to a day or weekend off. Spend a day or two doing absolutely no planning. Things won't fall apart in your absence. Go to a spa for the day and allow yourself to be pampered with a massage or a facial. You can return to the real world and planning with a refreshed, more positive outlook on the Bar/Bat Mitzvah. Also, don't be hesitant to ask family members for help. This is an enormous responsibility for you, and family members will be happy to assist you in planning for this momentous occasion.

Things may go wrong in the planning, but stay positive. Things are never as bad as they seem. Last minute problems and hitches will prove not so terrible if you maintain a feeling of positivity throughout the process. Don't allow yourself to become overwhelmed with feelings of anxiousness or despair. If you feel these emotions taking over, remove yourself from the situation as previously stated. Breaks are key to maintaining your sanity and usefulness throughout the planning process. Regardless of what happens during your planning, remember one thing. Nothing can go wrong that will take away from the true meaning of this event in your child's life. The reception might fall to pieces, but you will always have that video of your son or daughter reciting a section of the Torah. Never lose sight of the real meaning behind this event.

The Right Venue

An early but important step in planning a Bar or Bat Mitzvah is choosing the perfect venue. You will want the location to be fairly easily accessible to in-town guests. Try to find something close to your home. Are their hotels nearby for out of town guests to stay? Think about how comfortable the location will make your guests. After all, these people are taking a day to see you on this important occasion- don't make them drive six miles on a washboard dirt road just because you like a certain outdoor spot there. Don't choose someplace that doesn't fit you and your child's personalities, but at the same time, try to be reasonable.

If you are having a reception in a hall or at an outdoor venue which offers staff, find out what the establishment does. Determine ahead of time what services can be provided and at what extra cost. What is the venue's responsibility at your child's Mitzvah? Are they serving the food, organizing a wait staff, or doing anything? Also be sure to find out exactly what you are allowed to do. Some venues may want to do all of the table decorations and may not want outside materials used. Some venues will require you and your florist to take on all of the decorating yourself. Amount of service usually governs how much the venue costs. Determine how much service means to you versus the freedom to decorate yourself and the low cost. Many venues will have a well balanced combination of qualities.

Regardless of the amount of services which are provided or the cost, the staff at the location should be helpful and courteous to you. They should be respectful and take your concerns into consideration. They should answer phone calls, and return phone calls promptly.

They should reply quickly to emails, and not act in a manner as though they are trying to avoid you at all costs. Venues such as these will prove to be unreliable in the planning, and they will more than likely drop the ball on your big day. They will also misinform you but chalk it up to mistakes or miscommunications. Your venue staff should be clear and upfront, assisting you in any way which they can. Most have an event coordinator who should be in touch with you on a regular basis keeping you informed as the date draws closer.

The most important part of the venue is how you feel about it. Do you love it? Don't judge it in its barren state. Try to see it decorated with floral arrangements and bathed in candlelight. The venue may even allow you to stop by before a Bar/Bat Mitzvah held there and see the place all dressed up similarly to how it would be for yours. This is a helpful tool to see the potential of a room. If you can't do this, than try to be imaginative when viewing a venue. The most important part is that you and your child will be beaming as you walk into the room. Would this location make him or her beam?

Theme

You may or may not choose to have a theme for your child's Bar/Bat Mitzvah. Themes can be a fun outlet to have eclectic or different activities at the party. They can also be limiting if you select too narrow of a theme. Choose a theme that will make your child happy and there are endless possibilities. All that is required is time and creativity on your part. Think of how to intertwine your theme into every aspect of the celebration.

The theme should be something that your child enjoys. For example, if he or she is an athlete, you could do a sports theme. This would be enjoyable for your child and his or her friends. You can decorate the reception hall with sports equipment and posters of famous sports figures. Provide pool tables, Nerf balls, and other games. The dance floor can be taped to look like a basketball court. Be creative; you can have a lot of fun with this theme. As far as sweet snacks go, you can make cupcakes and brownies in the shapes of balls and hockey pucks.

For the avid music fan, you could plan a rock and roll themed Bar or Bat Mitzvah. The invitation can be shaped like a jukebox or even a record. Decorate the hall like a '50s diner, complete with jukebox and booths at which to eat. The obvious balloons and streamers are great decorations and fit the era perfectly. You can show the kids how to swing dance and have a great time dancing. The adults can have nice food while the kids will be happy with diner themed burgers and fries.

Another idea is to do a movie themed event. Take the Terminator movies for example. There are dozens of entertaining ways to incorporate this movie into your party. You could have a cut out of the Terminator for kids to have their picture taken with, as well as playing modern and techno music. Decorate the hall to look like it is made out of metal. You can post cutouts that look like robots to guard the hall entrance. You can also rent cutout props of destroyed tanks and cars strewn around the reception hall. What you don't make look like metal, you can decorate with a camouflage pattern.

There are many different ways to incorporate your theme into the most memorable and fun Bar/Bat Mitzvah possible for your child. What better way to celebrate your child than to theme the occasion after one of his or her favorite things? Let your imagination run wild for a themed party. Your child may suggest something that you think is too wild or far out, but anything can be tasteful if you go about it in the correct way. You can tone down a crazy idea or juice up a bland idea by using details properly. Either way, themed Bar/Bat Mitzvahs are a wonderful way to celebrate such an important occasion.

Going Green

A growing trend in the world is a move towards environmentalism. If your son or daughter is interested in nature, science, or just the outdoors in general, he or she might find it fun to do an eco themed event. You can decorate a hall to look like the outdoors, or you can even host the event at an outdoors location such as a park or beach. There are countless ways to infuse an eco-friendly theme into your event.

The setting for your green Bar/Bat Mitzvah is crucial. A park event would be very appropriate for such a theme or even a beach.   Your child could invite his/her friends out the weekend before to do a beach/park cleanup. It's a great way to include an eco-friendly activity without making people get messy on the actual day. Plus, you don't want a dirty event site anyways. Although weather is touchy, and you may need to dress according to heat or cold, outdoor events can be very fitting and very fun.

Most people opt for indoor Bar/Bat Mitzvahs even if simply for the unpredictable nature of weather. This is fine, and you can transform any venue into a green paradise with a little creativity. Bring small trees indoors in pots and place them around the facility. Set up a photo area where kids can be photographed hugging a tree. It will create laughter at the very least. With trees around, you can drape blue cloth on the ceiling and have forest green table cloths. The possibilities are endless for creating an outdoors oasis.

You will need to do more than simply create an outdoor or faux outdoors event to make it truly green. There are lots of different ways to incorporate sustainable practices in your Bar/Bat Mitzvah. Instead of providing disposable cameras on each table, set up one table with just a couple digital cameras. Disposables create waste, and that's not very green. Also, ensure that the venue is serving food on real dishes, no paper plates or plastic cups. Have recycling bins set up for people to dispose of their beverage bottles and cans. You can dress them up to match the décor, but the point is to encourage sustainable, eco-friendly behavior during the event. Another fun thing to do is to set up one food table that contains only all natural and organic foods. This will require some research on your part to learn how to make these foods. But you can make a veggie platter from locally grown or organic vegetables. Make snacks using only healthy and natural food products. People will be surprised at how good some of them taste.

Have a party that shows your guests that going green can be classy, elegant, and sensible. Don't be afraid to explain to people why you themed your party this way. You could even put up information stations about the earth, discussing different issues. This is a controversial topic among some, so be careful not to ruffle feathers with some guests. If done thoughtfully, this theme can be informational, fun, and rewarding.

Charity

If your child has a giving spirit, or you would like to teach him or her to have one, a Bar/Bat Mitzvah can be a great opportunity for growth. You can choose a worthy charitable organization to which to donate. The money gifts which your child receives can be given to this charity. Don't force your child to do this. It should seem to be the right thing to do in his/her eyes. Allow him or her to help research and pick out an organization to benefit from the Bar/Bat Mitzvah. This is a beautiful way to show your child, how he or she can bless others.

First of all, you cannot and should not force your son or daughter to give all of the money away. You can bring up the idea and gage how it is received. Give him/her a while to think about it; you can expect hesitation. If the child decides to do this project and help an organization, then you can move forward with selecting a worthy cause. Do not push the issue, however, if it is not well received. The child will gain nothing from the experience if he or she does not want to do it.

Once you have selected a charity, you can begin planning on how to incorporate this charity into your event. It's a good idea to inform guests on the invitation where their gifts will be going. This can be done tastefully with something like, "David has graciously chosen to donate any monies received to such and such organization." At any rate, guests need to be made aware that your child will not be keeping the money received. Otherwise, he or she will have to deal with relatives asking what he or she is going to buy with it.

In addition to the notice on the invitation, you can incorporate the charity into your event on the big day. Have a table or booth set up somewhere that it will not conflict with your colors or theme. Provide a description of the charity with some pictures. Set up a box for people to put their donations, similar to a card box for a wedding. This display can be in conjunction with the gift table or separate; it's up to you.

If your child does indeed go through with this charity project, be sure to praise him or her. You might reward him or her with a present or trip that they've been wanting. Get him/her a present or take him/her to a theme park for the day. In any fashion, be sure to reward your child in some manner for his or her selfless efforts. If you reward this kind of behavior at this age, it will only foster more and more giving as he or she grows older. Help to grow a generous spirit in your child; benefiting a charity with this Bar/Bat Mitzvah is a perfect way to do it.

Music

Music is key to ensuring any Bar Mitzvah or Bat Mitzvah is a success. Hiring a DJ and entertainers is rapidly becoming a more popular custom when hosting these events.

A good DJ with party motivators is key to making your Bar Mitzvah even more memorable. The motivators should encourage interaction with guests and be entertaining. The MC should be able to collaborate a grand entrance for your son or daughter, introduce the first dance and coordinate any dance to be done on the big day. The DJ should also be able to provide meal service music and video production sound re-enforcement. They should coordinate any candle light songs and assist with the ceremony.

Ensure that the DJ has a music line up that will be enjoyable for all ages. There should be a variety of different music tastes as to cater for the needs of all your guests. It is important that the DJ is prepared for any dedication and has a dance mix of the hora.

Hiring dancers for your Bar Mitzvah or Bat Mitzvah is a great way you can keep the children, who are attending your the occasion, entertained. The dancers should dance with the children as well as the adults. The dance performer/team should be in control of the events taking place on the dance floor throughout the day. By keeping popular dances such as the conga-line, Jewish folk dancing and the Macarena, you include all your guests and encourage them to participate.

You can assign a particular dancer to dance only with the children while the other dancers entertain the adults. The dancers who are entertaining the children can do simple dances and the children can copy them. This is a great way to keep the little ones entertained while their parents are free to enjoy this marvelous day with adult entertainment.

You can also hire a party band instead of a DJ. Ensure that the band is familiar with Jewish tradition and music. The band should be able to entertain the guest, in a similar way as a DJ. The band's music should be suitable for all ages. It is always a good idea to hold auditions and listen to a couple of bands before deciding which band is going to play at the Bar Mitzvah or Bat Mitzvah. Warn the band against any special requests and suggest that they bring a few CD's containing popular dance music.

One can always hire a DJ and a live band. This will provide the perfect balance between two worlds and offer your guest a wider variety of music. Incorporating both a DJ and a live band will also compensate for different tastes in music. You can alternate between the band and the DJ throughout the day. Meet with the band and the DJ before the event to confirm their duties and when they will be performing.

Remember to provide something for the entertainers to eat and to drink. Have breaks during the program where the entertainers can rest and eat. This will ensure a happy staff and cause less stress on the big day.

DJ vs. Live

As you plan for a Bar/Bat Mitzvah, you may find yourself debating over what kind of musical style you would like to present. Is it a black tie event that would be well suited for live music? Or would you rather hire a DJ who the kids would find more enjoyable. Both bands and disc jockeys have their positive and negative aspects. The trick is to select music that is most properly matched for your specific event and theme. You will also want to consider how age appropriate the music will be for the children. Obviously, they will have less appreciation for a string quartet than the adults would.

DJs can be a great part of your special day. You will need to find a good one in a virtual sea of bad ones. The key is word of mouth reputation. Talk to other people who have used a DJ for their Bar/Bat Mitzvahs. Also, your venue may have some ideas. Often times the event planner at your venue will know of local disc jockeys who have worked at events there. He or she will have an idea of who is good and who is not so good. They may even recommend a personal favorite. Whether or not you take the advice, the worst mistake you can make is to hire someone with a bad reputation or no reputation at all. If nobody has heard of a particular DJ, there is probably a reason for this. The good part about DJs is that they are flexible on what style of music your family and guests enjoy whether it is hip hop or country. DJs are also beneficial because of their ability to play to the crowd and really get your guests involved. There is a certain level of sophistication which cannot be achieved except by live music. DJs usually cost less, however, and can be more personalized to the event than bands.

Live music, as previously stated, provides an aura to an event that a DJ booth cannot recreate. Live music is more impressive to guests often times, and the sound quality is different and some would say better. Live bands have an overall better appeal than disc jockeys because live music is often viewed as more upscale, and because so many DJs are terrible. Live music might also suit your theme. If you are doing a Middle Eastern, "Arabian Nights" theme, than live music could be very appropriate, and a DJ would not be able to do justice to snake charm type of music. Live music is usually more expensive than disc jockeys, and often times the bands are specialized and only perform one style of music. A DJ would better be able to blend different musical tastes to make everyone happy.

Whether you choose a disc jockey or a live band, do your research. Don't allow someone to perform at such an important occasion unless they are loaded with positive recommendations. Music can really make or break your event. Weigh your options thoughtfully and make a decision that will make you, your child, and your guests happy.

ADJA.org

DJKJ.com

Catering

Finding a caterer that will cater for the needs of you and your guests is also key to a successful Bar Mitzvah or Bat Mitzvah.

When choosing a caterer for your Bar Mitzvah ensure that they are prepared for any guests who are vegetarians or who may have special diets. If you know of guests who do have any special dietary requirements you must inform your caterer. Many guests are sensitive to sugar and caffeine. Ensure that the caterer provides sugar free and low calorie drinks, such as: Diet cola.

If you have a set seating plan, try to seat your guests as far from the DJ, music and loud speakers as possible. If your affair is less formal and you do not have a seating plan, place the tables as far away from the music as possible.

It is seldom that all the people who RSVP show up at the event. Keeping this in mind you can save money by telling the caterer to prepare for at least 95% of the amount of people you have on your guest list.

You can arrange with the florist or the caterer to transport the flowers from the ceremony to the venue of the party. You can also ask the caterer to arrange the flowers on the tables.

When choosing a caterer for your Bar Mitzvah or Bat Mitzvah, one should consider as many different companies as possible and choose the one you feel best suits your taste and occasion. Ask for quotes and compare them to your budget. Choose the one you feel most comfortable with. Collect quotations from caterers before deciding on a budget. This will give you a general idea of the price and allow you to create a realistic and practical budget.

Confirm with the caterer at least three days before the event. Make sure that the company has the correct time and date. Ensure everything is in order for the big day.

If you are serving a buffet always ensure that there are enough napkins and inquire if the catering service is responsible for cleaning up after the event.

Keep it simple. One can easily go overboard with catering. Keep the catering simple and enjoyable for everyone. When deciding on the menu make sure that the food is suitable for children and adults. Try to avoid food that spicy, etc.

Ensure that the caterer has your contact details so they can inform you if there are ant problems or if they have any questions. You should also keep the contact details of the catering service so you can contact them if you wish to make any changes to the menu, etc.

Photography

You'll want to treasure the moments of your child's Bar/Bat Mitzvah forever. Long after the party, you will have the photographs to remind you of that special day. You need to take several measures to ensure that you have great photos that capture every important moment. You should hire a photographer, but there are less obvious ways to get great photos in addition to your photographer's pictures. Indeed, you can never have too many pictures of such a joyous and important event in your child's life.

First of all, you will need to hire a good quality photographer to document the event from start to finish. He or she should arrive before the ceremony begins and follow you until the end of the reception. Your photographer should provide you with samples of his or her work. Price does not always reflect quality of work. The most important considerations for quality are sample work and word of mouth reputation. If he or she is the best photographer in the world, but shows up late or not at all to your event, than it does you know good. Find someone with a solid reputation as a talented and reliable photographer.

Another great idea to get lots of great candid photos is to place a disposable camera at each table at the party. In this manner you will get pictures of your guests enjoying themselves. You will also probably get some nice candid photos of your son or daughter, as all eyes will be on him/her.

In addition, you will be providing your guests with some entertainment that benefits you. People love to take pictures – especially catching each other in embarrassing moments, such as food on their faces. These photos will make great memories in the future. Just be certain to specify on the camera or on a card near the camera that the cameras are to be left on the table at the end of the night. Then, simply collect the cameras and have them developed.

A few weeks after the Bar/Bat Mitzvah, make some phone calls or emails and find out if your relatives and friends have any good photos from the event taken with their own cameras. If they do, you can ask if they will kindly send you copies if it was a film camera. If they used a digital camera, they can email them to you or burn them to a CD to give or send to you. Then, of course, thank them graciously for the photos.

Invitations

Invitations are an important part of any party or event. For a Bar/Bat Mitzvah, the invitations can reflect your child, your faith, or your theme. If your child enjoys ballet, send ballet slipper invitations or soccer ball ones if he/she is a soccer player or fan. You can also fit the invitation to the theme of the event. If you are themeing it after a movie, have the invitations resemble some item of the movie, like the ring or sword of *Lord of the Rings*. You can also have invitations with a religious, spiritual meaning to them. The invitations should be of good quality and reflect some individuality.

Invitations should be sent early in advance to allow time for responses. Your caterer and venue will want a final head count by two weeks before the day. Therefore, the most ideal time to send your invitations is eight weeks before the date. Any earlier and guests may not be sure of their plans; any later and people will have made plans, and will not get their replies to you in time. Include with each invitation an RSVP card with self addressed stamped envelope and a reception card.

You may wonder what date to place as a deadline for your RSVP cards. Most offer a phrase such as "please reply by blank," or "the pleasure of a reply is requested by blank." This can be tricky. You want to give your guests enough time to figure out their plans so that as many as possible can make it, but you need as much time as possible yourself to deal with vendors once you have a final head count. Another point is that unfortunately many people don't take RSVP dates seriously and will send them late. The earlier that your date is, the more time you'll have to deal with stragglers. Ideally, you should set the date at three weeks before the event, and no later than two weeks before. If you send your invites at eight weeks, this gives your guests a month to decide if they are coming and to return the RSVP cards.

You will undoubtedly receive RSVP cards several days after your deadline. Some may even get them back to you a week or more late. Should you punish them for their tardiness and tell them no, or welcome them? Punishing friends and relatives is never a very good solution to this inconsiderate behavior. You may be furious at a cousin's audacity to return the RSVP card with a "yes" two weeks past the deadline, but try to maintain some degree of civility. This is your child's party, and not an opportunity to feud with relatives. However, if you don't punish your relative with a "no," then you are punishing your venue and caterer by forcing changes late in the planning- past their deadline. If you need to make last minute changes to your guest list, be sure to be respectful when dealing with your vendors; they have schedules too. Be kind and apologetic; explain the situation. Most will understand if they've been in the business for any length of time.

Non-Jewish Invites

You may wonder how your gentile friends will feel during your child's sacred day. Depending upon how many other Jewish friends that they have, they may not have attended a Bar/Bat Mitzvah ever before. You should not exclude people from the invite list just because they are not Jewish. They will exercise respect for the occasion even if they do not know a thing about what is going on. You will want them to feel comfortable among your other friends and family. You can take some measures to ensure that they have as great a time celebrating as all of your other Jewish guests do.

One thing you can do that is always nice is to include in your ceremony program a brief summary of what a Bar/Bat Mitzvah is. Explain the historical and spiritual significance of the event, and why it is important in the life of your specific child. Guests can read this before the ceremony begins, and will not be as lost as to why this occasion is so important. Often times people do not have any knowledge of cultures and religions different from their own. Don't hold this against them. Instead try to inform them. Don't provide excessive information, but enough to help them to understand the ceremony's importance.

Try to be patient with your guests as they may have many questions. Non-Jewish friends may bombard you with inquiries once they arrive at the reception venue. They will doubtless want to know what everything which occurred at the ceremony means, and why it was done. An insert in your program will help to alleviate many simple questions, but guests will still pester you. Be patient and polite. Answer their questions as best as you can. If it becomes a nuisance, simply tell them, "I would love to explain to you all about our child's Bar/Bat Mitzvah, but tonight, I'd really like to just celebrate. Maybe we could talk another time about it?" Generally people will lay off on the questioning if you politely ask them to.

The most important part of having non-Jewish guests at your child's Bar/Bat Mitzvah is to make sure that they feel welcome. Chances are that they will already be feeling very self conscious. If it is a first Bar/Bat Mitzvah, especially, they will certainly be worried about properly conducting themselves. Be sure to offer help with things like Yamakas to those who need assistance in wearing them properly. Little things like this will help your guests to feel more comfortable. They will feel like they fit in better, and will therefore have a better time. Be kind and polite when dealing with even the simplest minded questions. Issues that may seem common sense to you might be completely foreign to your guests. Practice patience and kindness, and soon all of your guests will be having a fabulous time. Once they are happy, you can enjoy the occasion as well.

Seating Arrangements

Often times, people face a dilemma when it comes to drawing up a seating chart. It always seems to work out that in making one table happy, you will make another unhappy. More than likely, people will be coming to this event who don't like each other but like you. Family members may be at odds, and other groups of people may simply not have much in common.

Your first priority should be to separate any people who truly dislike each other. If you know that these people hate one another, then don't sit them together. Unless you are looking for problems, keep enemies apart, with a table in between preferably. You may need to mix up the families or groups of friends for this to happen. It will be worth it not to have a feud destroy your child's big day. Hopefully your friends will be civilized enough to hold their fire until the parking lot at any rate. It's generally not a good idea to invite two people who hate each other this much, but if you love both of them, there's not much else you can do. They are bound to bump into each other once or twice, but you should do your part to prevent them from spending any more time with each other at dinner. Unless you force unnecessary contact, your fighting friends should be gracious and civilized throughout the occasion.

Your next goal once these folks are separated should be to group family members by relation and friendliness. Try to keep people together who are already close. Keep in town relatives together, and out of town relatives together. This said, you may want to merge in town and out of towners together if it is a close connection, say parents and children, of which one has moved away. This event is a great chance for them to catch up and re-connect if they haven't seen each other in awhile.

Your final task, once you have taken care of fighting friends and relatives, is to seat the rest of your guests. Try to create groups of people who have things in common. For example, seat parents of your kids' classmates together. Even if they don't know each other yet, they will already have a great deal to talk about considering that their children attend school together. Your child can help you with this part of the seating arrangement. He/she will know which kids get along with which other kids, and whose parents are better friends than others.

Wait until the week of your event to compile your seating chart. Late RSVPs have a tendency of ruining a beautifully laid out arrangement. Don't stress out too much, because people will move around during the party, this is really only a dinner seating chart. If people have problems  with each other than they can separate. Chances are, if these people are your friends and care about you, they won't risk ruining your child's day with their own issues. Once people get relaxing and dancing, everyone will have a great time regardless of who they are sitting with.

Decorations

People planning large events generally face one of two problems. Sometimes the budget does not hold enough to adequately decorate the venue. On the other extreme, some parents go overboard, spending far too much on decorations, and making the room appear tacky and overdone. Both of these situations are relatively simple to fix if you adapt the correct mindset. The first problem is even easier to remedy than the second because budget is often more curable than taste.

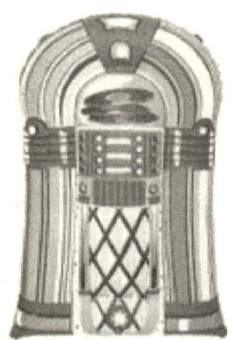

If you are dealing with limited funds for decorations, don't worry. You don't need showy floral centerpieces at every table. Flowers are the most expensive form of decorations; all you need is some creativity. Take into account the theme of the event. If it's a rock and roll theme, you could create a display using old vinyl records, big sunglasses and sequins as a tribute to "the king." You might set up little fake juke boxes at each table. Candles are a cheaper alternative to flowers as well, and can be great if they fit with your theme. Bowls filled with water, with floating tea lights create a beautiful ambiance. You could also arrange varying sized pillar candles in the center of each table for a simple yet elegant centerpiece. Themed occasions offer more room for variety in centerpieces, as you can turn just about anything into a decoration, from basketballs to ballet slippers.

If you've got a lot of dough to work with, but aren't quite sure how to best use it, the best thing to do is to keep things elegant and tasteful. If you want chiffon draped from the ceiling, than do it tastefully and in keeping with the colors and theme of the event. Sheer is always a subtle way to do draperies. You don't want to feel too trapped by all one color. If you have a bold color like red this is especially true. Red draperies, tablecloths, napkins, and flowers would be too overpowering. Use an accent color to mix things up a bit. Your floral arrangements should reflect the feeling of your theme. If you are having a dance themed party, soft pink roses and white calla lilies might be the perfect combination to reflect the delicateness. If you are doing a disco themed party, bright colors are the way to go. Choose two colors as your main ones such as orange and purple, but you can include other colored flowers in your arrangements to keep them interesting. The more exotic the theme you have, the more exotic your flowers should be. You don't want red roses for a luau party; you would need more tropical flowers.

Your decorations can be as showy or simple as you envision them to be. Keep one rule of thumb in mind: "everything in moderation." Don't allow yourself to get carried away, but neither should you feel limited by your budget if you don't have a lot. All that it takes to pull of breathtaking decorations is a little creativity and taste.

Party Favors

Traditionally the host of a large party, such as that following a Bar/Bat Mitzvah, will provide little favors for the guests. You can choose to incorporate your theme into your favors, provide a poem written by or about your child on his/her day, or any number of things. You can also take a less traditional approach to providing gifts for your guests.

If you are a fan of tradition and would like each guest to take home a small memento, there are countless options. The first most common choice is to provide edible treats for guests to take home. You can make cute little baggies filled with the treat of your choice. Tie the baggies with a color coordinating ribbon and set one at each place setting. That is a simple solution to this traditional obligation. More creative options could be bookmarks set at each place with a poem written about the child on it. You could also buy little wallet sized frames and put a picture of your child in each one, and set them up at the tables. You can also provide themed gifts. If your event is sports themed, you could provide little soccer ball key chains at each place setting, or something such as that.

If you are comfortable with the idea of not everyone receiving a gift, you can use some other ideas. If you have floral centerpieces, you can give these as gifts. Obviously there is not one for everyone, so choose randomly. Place a token under one chair at each table at random. The lucky person in that seat can claim the prize. Just inform your DJ of this plan so that he can tell your guests when to look for the token. For a token you can use a penny or a flower petal or anything really as long as it fits discretely.

If you don't have floral centerpieces and/or don't want to give away what you do have, you can use another technique. Make a list of things that you are willing to give away like decorations, props, flower arrangements, etc... Then have your guests fill out slips of paper with their names on them to drop into a bowl. At some point during the event, your DJ can draw names for the different prizes.

There are pros and cons to each option. With larger gifts, most guests walk away with nothing. However, with little trinket gifts for everyone, chances are it will get lost or thrown away. If it is edible, it will be eaten and forgotten. Large gifts provide a few random guests with a piece of memorabilia, while smaller ones provide everyone with a sense of inclusion. The choice is yours, and nobody's feelings will be hurt regardless of what you choose to do. Guests will be thrilled with the occasion itself and will not feel bad about any party favor situation.

A Great Novelty Resource:
http://OutsideTheBox.MakesParties.com

Child Responsibilities

The Bar/Bat Mitzvah is a celebration for your son or daughter after all, and he/she needs to take on some responsibility for the planning of the event. You cannot be expected to do everything in addition to caring for your home and working. Your child will probably enjoy the opportunity to have input concerning the decisions about the party. Some kids will gladly sit back and watch you do everything, while others will feel left out if they do not get to help. At any rate, your child should shoulder some of the responsibilities.

The first obvious area in which you really cannot help your child is the learning of the Torah. He/she must learn the section alone, and you cannot learn it for him/her. You can however, ensure that your child begins practicing far enough in advance. You may need to nag, and your son/daughter may become unhappy with you. But, he or she is going to be far more unhappy on the big day when he/she faces embarrassment in front of friends and family. Try to explain to your child why it is so important to learn the Torah, and why they should begin practicing and not wait until the last minute. Threatening them with this horror of embarrassment might help to do the trick.

Another area where your child can be of help is in the guest list. You may think that you don't want there help in this area- that you want to decide who is invited. Step out of the driver's seat for a moment and remember that you want your child to have a happy day. Let him or her contribute to the guest list, and don't only invite kids of parents whom you like. Always keep in mind whom you are planning this party for, and who needs to have a smile on his or her face. Put your preferences aside when it comes to the children on the guest list.

One thing that kids have a lot of that parents often lack is creativity. Get your child's opinion on decorations, theme ideas and color schemes. If they suggest hot pink and lime green, you may need to exercise a parental veto. But most of the time kids have great suggestions to make, and they'll be excited to help pick things out. Utilize his or her eagerness to your advantage and be careful not to squash their enthusiasm with negativity.

Regardless of how your child helps, be sure to get them involved in some manner of the planning. Your son or daughter needs to feel like they have a say in what kind of party that they have. Even if it is only a minute part of it, let them have something. You'll find that kids can offer more help than trouble in planning this kind of party.

Activities for the Kids

Keeping your child and his or her friends entertained is essential at the Bar/Bat Mitzvah event. Bored kids will become unruly, not to mention irritating to the adults. Your child will also be displeased with the party if your budget skimps on entertainment, or if that is where your imagination stops. Any event without fun entertainment is a drag, but with all the children at the party, you need to be extra certain that you have plenty of things to occupy them with.

There are plenty of ways to provide entertainment if you have a large budget from which to plan. There are the obvious choices of entertainers such as magicians and people with trained animals. There may be limitations on animals depending upon your particular venue. Although a magician seems a simple way to solve it, a good one can be a wonderful asset to the event. A good DJ is a basic necessity to ensure a lively atmosphere also. Your DJ can make or break the party. He or she should have great word of mouth reviews; that's the best way to find a good one. Your DJ should not simply play music. He or she should play an active role in getting your guests involved in dancing and keeping the mood perky.

There are also some less obvious ways to provide fun for your guests. You can hire a caricature artist to draw humorous pictures of the guests. Another idea is to get an artist to give the kids henna or airbrushed tattoos. An oxygen bar is an easy option as well that kids today love. Services like these are good because the workers provide entertainment only to those who want it. You don't have to deal wit some unpleasant child complaining about the "stupid magician" or the "lousy singer." The children can choose for themselves what they would like to do.

If you are working from a tight budget, there are equally fun solutions to entertainment. The difference is that the tighter your budget is, the more creative you will need to be. Contests are an easy way to occupy the kids' attention for awhile. Although you can conduct these contests yourself, you will need to buy prizes to offer the winners; kids won't play for the joy of winning. Use your imagination for other activities that connect to your theme. If you have a '70s theme, teach the children how to disco. Karaoke is another fun way to get the guests involved in something fun and inexpensive.

When dealing with your child's special day, you want to make certain that he or she and his/her friends have a fun time. You also want to save yourself and adult guests the stress of dealing with difficult or antsy children. Planning does not need to be difficult. Even if you are not the most creative person, you can think of plenty of imaginative solutions by light research and talking to people who have already planned Bar/Bat Mitzvahs. Doubtless, with a little effort, your child will have a wonderful and memorable day shared with family and friends.

Tips for the Kids

Everyone knows that adult taste and kid taste do not always match up. In fact, it is a rarity when they do. Bar/Bat Mitzvahs are difficult to plan in that the party is meant to please both your child and his/her friends as well as please adult relatives and friends. As much as you want the event to be classy and tasteful, there are certain elements which need to be geared toward making the younger crowd happy.

Food is such an important part of any occasion. Making the food kid friendly does not mean reducing the cuisine to hot dogs and hamburgers for all. Simply offer a variety of dishes, some of which will appeal toward the children. Provide grown up food for the adults, and kid food for the kids; it's only fair. In the same way, you should make sodas and other kid friendly drinks available as well. They won't be satisfied with just water.

As for music, it should be fun and lively that young and old alike can dance to. If you have a DJ, encourage him to play a variety of music. Don't overwhelm the older group with excessive rap or rock, but include a little bit to make the kids happy. Everybody can have fun dancing to a lot of older music. Think era circa 1960's-1980's. There is a lot of "please all" type of music to be found in this time period- everything from Elvis and The Beatles to 80's rock. This music is soft enough for the older people and fun enough for kids.

Aside from food and music, other forms of entertainment should exist for the kids during the event. Unfortunately pin the tail on the donkey doesn't work very well at this age. You will need to employ more high tech means of entertainment. If the kids get too bored they may get into trouble, or worse get you into trouble with your vendors. You might consider an oxygen bar. This is a safe way to keep the kids amused and behaving themselves. You can also set up a photo booth and offer props or character cut-outs for the kids to pose with. Another great way to get the kids involved in the party is to hire dancers. The dancers will provide the guests with something to look at. But in addition to that, they will encourage the kids and adults to get up and start dancing.

Your child's Bar/Bat Mitzvah is a celebration of him or her. Always keep this in mind as you plan. Don't allow yourself to become carried away with making good impressions on relatives or friends. As long as your child has fun, you should consider the event a success.

Try to remember the reason for the celebration during all of the commotion.

Bar/Bat Mitzvah Attire

The special young person who is starring in this ceremony should be dressed accordingly. A girl should wear a beautiful dress reflecting both the sanctity of the ceremony and joy of the celebration. The colors can compliment the color scheme and theme of the reception. Depending upon the individual regulations, dresses need to be of a certain level of modesty. Appropriate attire is expected of the young lady without ignoring her personal taste. Parents should keep this in mind when shopping. Shop well in advance for your dress— about six months. This allows for plenty of time for good selection and alterations to be made if necessary. As for hair, makeup, and jewelry, keep it in her taste and also age appropriate. She is a young lady now, but should not be allowed to look inappropriate by any means.

For a Bar Mitzvah, a young man should wear a nicely tailored suit. When purchasing a suit, keep in mind that boys grow rapidly at this age, so make sure that there is an ample hem to allow for alterations. You can also wait until the day gets closer, but don't wait too long. Be sure to double check the fit a few weeks before the big day. You don't want your boy to have shin length pants at such an important occasion. You may also need to rent or purchase a tuxedo for the reception, depending upon the formality of the event.

As a parent, you should also dress appropriately. Mothers should dress nicely with appropriate formality. There is a tendency for some mothers to overdress rather than under dress. Understanding the significance of the event, some moms will go all out with a beautiful dress and jewelry, and hair done up fancily. You do not, however, want to outshine your daughter in any circumstances. Keep in mind that this is her day, and she should be the focal point of your guests' attentions. Spend the energy that you would preening yourself in helping your daughter get ready. Do her hair nicely, or have it done by a professional stylist. If you want to have your hair done as well, keep with something simple, so that you do not distract from the star of the day.

A Bar/Bat Mitzvah is a serious event in your child's life. The ceremony should be treated with respect and sincerity. Don't let this importance hinder your wardrobe. This is a celebration, and you should dress accordingly. Be formal but festive. Don't be too over-the-top as to look like you're seeking attention, but don't sport a boring outfit either. Let the joy that you feel inside about this wonderful occasion radiate outward in your choice of attire.

Hairstyles

If you are wondering how to do your daughter's hair for her Bat Mitzvah, or your own hair for your son's Bar Mitzvah, there are several tips that you should keep in mind. The first thing to remember is face shape. Make sure that your hair is flattering to your face. Also, keep within the theme of the party. An over the top "do" might not be fitting for a sports themed event. If you find yourself conflicted, always go with less rather than more.

Before deciding upon a hairstyle for this occasion, take a moment to sit in front of the mirror. Pull your hair back and look at your face. Is it oval, meaning longer than wide. Oval faces have the tendency to look long and narrow if the hair is not styled to flatter. With an oval face, you will want to keep away from updos that pile your hair onto the top of your head. A pile of hair on top of your head will make an already oval shaped face appear even longer. Instead have the hair pulled back toward the center of the back of your head and styled from that position.

If your face is more round or square, meaning that it is equal in length and width, than you will take a different approach than oval faced individuals. With this shaped face, you will benefit from updos that make your face look a little longer. If you choose to wear your hair down, keep away from over the top curls. If you make the hair on the sides of your head seem bigger, your face will appear even wider. Try a sleeker style with clean lines to add length to your face.

You might have a scar, bruise, or other imperfection on your face, neck, or other exposed area of skin. Often times your hair can be styled in a manner as to hide this blemish. If it cannot be hidden, hair, if positioned properly, can effectively distract from it. Use your hair to your advantage. It can help you to highlight all of your best features, while at the same time, covering up the less attractive flaws.

Style your hair to fit the theme and atmosphere of the event. Just as you wouldn't wear a ball gown if the event had a rock and roll theme, don't allow yourself to get carried away on an intricate hairstyle if it will clash with your outfit, the room, and the other guests. Having your hair done professionally can be a big help to you. Many stylists are talented, qualified, and don't charge too much. You can tell your stylist what you envision for the overall effect. Show her your dress or outfit, and explain your theme. Generally, a good stylist will be able to pinpoint a style that is just right for you. Share your ideas for what you'd like your hair to look like, but don't disallow your stylist from helping you. Hair is her job, and it can be insulting if you don't let her do her job. She has your best interest in mind.

While at the event, forget about your hair. It is bound to change from its original perfection. Curls will relax a bit and volume will shrink. Don't panic. You'll still be beautiful, and the point then is to have a good time. Don't ruin it for yourself by trying to fix your hair. The point of a hairstyle is to make you feel good not bad after all.

Make-up

Special occasion make-up is not like daily make-up; it is an entirely different animal. You will doubtlessly need to alter your current habits to make the most of your face for this event. People generally fall into one of three categories: those who don't wear make-up, or very little; those who wear an appropriate amount for daily wear, and those who prefer a dramatic look all the time. Each one of these types of habits presents a conflict to make-up for a special occasion.

You may hardly ever wear makeup- a dash of lip color once in awhile. If you're one of these, than you will need to step up your game for this occasion. Even if you have great skin, you'll need make-up to maximize your features. There will be many photos taken of you, and make-up will help with shine control, as well as help to really make your face "pop" in those pictures. If you fail to wear any make-up, you will blend into the crowd. Although your child is the star of the day, you'll want people to notice you as not just another guest.

If you are not in the habit of wearing make-up, you will want to consult someone else. Hire someone to do your make-up for you, or ask a friend to help you. Your child's Bar/Bat Mitzvah is not, however, the best time to learn how to do makeup.

If you are in the habit of wearing make-up on a regular basis, you will want to amp it up a bit for such a special occasion. The same old daytime look that you normally wear is going to be too bland for such an event. Create a more dramatic eye, and use a slightly bolder lip color. Don't be tempted to do clown make-up, but rev things up from how you typically would apply them. If you are used to doing make-up, you probably don't need a professional's help, but it never hurts. So if it's important to you, than go for it.

If you're make-up habits include a daily use of fuchsia and/or lime green, you will definitely need to scale back for this occasion. It's really not so much about lessening your make-up as changing how you apply. Use color, but use it appropriately. Coordinate with your outfit as well as your skin tone. If you follow these guidelines, your make-up can be fun and intense without looking overdone and ridiculous. You may think that because you have experience with make-up, you don't need any assistance. It might be hard to break your old habits, so the use of a professional could be just what you need to make sure that everything looks perfect for this big day.

Gift Ideas

A Bar/Bat Mitzvah is a great way to give a child gifts that are meaningful and carry spiritual significance. You can give a family tree so that he/she will understand the personal importance of his or her history. Another way to convey this importance is to give some sort of family heirloom. The child will then better understand his or her value within the family. He or she will know how important he/she is to you and to the whole family to be given a gift of sentimental value. Books and videos about Jewish history and tradition also make excellent ways of transferring important meanings to any child. Prayer books, too, are excellent Bar/Bat Mitzvah gifts.

Other gifts of spiritual significance could include a Menorah or a Mezuzah to hang on the child's door. A Kiddush Cup and Shabbat candlesticks also make good gifts for the child who has just had his/her Bar/Bat Mitzvah. You can also give a storage box for decorative memorabilia from the occasion. A nice frame would be thoughtful with a picture of that special child. Jewelry such as bracelets and pendants of a spiritual theme also are beautiful gifts to give, and they will always remind the child of his/her heritage when he/she wears them.

If you choose to buy as gift that does not have Jewish spiritual significance, it is perfectly acceptable. You can choose to give cash, but there are also plenty of other fun things to buy. You can purchase the latest electronics, DVDs or CDs. Cool clothing is also always appreciated by kids of this age. If you have no idea what to buy, there is still another alternative besides cash. Get a gift certificate or card to one of the child's favorite stores. This can be a clothing store, an electronic store like Best Buy, or a bath and beauty product store for a girl. Go wherever you think that the individual child would most appreciate it.

Use cash gifts as a last resort, as they tend to lack personal thought. When purchasing a gift for your child or someone else's, try to always keep in mind the child's interests. While spiritual gifts are nice and highly appropriate on such an occasion, try to also incorporate an aspect that he/she would like about the gift. If you are passing on a precious family heirloom that the child may not fully appreciate until later, include a $20 gift card to somewhere fun so that he or she has something to enjoy more immediately. This is only fitting, because kids of this age are not likely to grasp the importance of many traditional gifts. In any case, put thought and time into your gift selection for such a momentous occasion, and the child will certainly be thrilled with your selection.

Be Happy

Don't worry; be happy.   It really is as simple as that. You need to stay cheerful during the planning of the event as well as the day of the Bar/Bat Mitzvah. As a parent, your attitude will have an impact on how your child feels about his or her day. It's also advisable to keep a happy demeanor for your own sanity. The less you worry, and the happier you are, the easier planning will be.

First of all, if you are a complaining, irritable mess during the planning of the Bar/Bat Mitzvah, your attitude will rub off on your child. He or she may take up a similar attitude acting angry and spoiled. On the other hand, he or she might think that you are not happy about the Bar Mitzvah. He/she might misconstrue your frustration, thinking that they (your child) are not worth the planning. He or she may believe that the event is really only a pain and extra hassle for family members. You don't ever want your child to feel guilty about having a Bar/Bat Mitzvah. Therefore, you need to keep up a cheerful attitude during the planning as well as the day of the occasion.

Another reason to be happy is for your own mental health. It's harder to be stressed out when you are happy, and it's harder to be happy when you are stressed out. So even if you have to lie to yourself, do it to keep up your spirit. You will be able to function much better if you are not miserable because one thing did not go according to plan. Planning the Bar/Bat Mitzvah will be stressful enough, so don't allow a poor attitude to compile and make things seem even worse.

You may wonder how you can possibly be happy all of the time when all you are doing is planning and stressing and worrying. Well, that's the problem. Take time away from all of the headaches. Remove yourself from the situation if it is causing you to be unhappy. Make room in your schedule to have fun with your family. Don't limit your time with your child to strictly Bar/Bat Mitzvah planning activities. Do normal fun activities as well. This will help both of you to unwind and relax. At the same time, it provides for excellent bonding time for the family. You may be toting your child to different venues and taking him or her shopping for an outfit after school frequently. This can ware down any relationship fairly easily. So instead, pick him or her up after school one day for dinner, or to see a newly released movie that he/she has been wanting to see. Remember to leave time in your schedule to enjoy your child, your family, and yourself. This attitude will be of great help when you need to tackle difficult matters in your planning.

On the Big Day

So the big day has come. You are feeling thrilled, proud, excited, and absolutely panicked about everything coming together. First of all relax; you are no good to anyone as a bundle of nerves. Start the morning off like you normally would. Call your caterer, venue, and all others who are involved from your house before you leave for the ceremony. Simply verify that all is going as planned. Do something special for your son or daughter as this is his/her special day from start to finish. Enjoy the morning, and look forward to the event.

Pack along your cell phone as you head off to the Temple. Remember to put it on silent during the ceremony. Nothing could be more dreadful than the caterer calling and interrupting during your child's recitation of the Torah. Don't allow your mistake to be the only/biggest mishap of the day. You will need to check your voice mail after the ceremony. This can be done on your way to the reception hall. Ten to one nobody will call and there will be no problems. Generally speaking if everything is on track in the morning, there will not be any serious problems other than the inevitable possible traffic delays for people. If there are any issues, however, you will want them to be resolved before your guests begin to arrive.

Once you get to the place of the party and you confirm that all of your vendors are present and prepared, you can breathe a sigh of relief. Now it's time to pay any that you have not paid in full yet. Have with you marked envelopes with the money for each vendors or entertainers. This makes it simple to discretely hand the named envelope to each of the people. Once you have done this, your work is complete. It is now time to kick back and have some fun. You've planned and prepped, working hard to make this day a success. Enjoy yourself.

As you and your son or daughter are the hosts of the party, you have an obligation to visit with people. The easiest way to do this is during the meal. People will be eating, and you will be less likely to get tied down talking to one long winded person. Simply make the rounds, stopping at each table to chat for three or four minutes. Simply ask if everyone is enjoying themselves, although it's obvious that they will be with all of your preparation. A good way to wrap up your chat is with, "Well, I'll let you get back to your meal..." This is why doing it at the meal time is so convenient. Your child, too, should make an attempt to visit with people, especially the adults. His or her obligation is not as socially mandatory as yours, however. Your child should have fun at the Bar/Bat Mitzvah, and family and friends will understand this

Don't Forget

There are certain things that you can't get done ahead of time, whether because of time constraint or whatever reason. On the big day, your main focus should be having fun, but a few details should not be overlooked. You've got to think about last minute décor preparations, business deals with vendors, as well as your own appearance. It's hard on the day of this occasion not to become swept away by the emotions and excitement. Therefore, plan ahead, and make a to-do list of what needs to be done on the day of the Bar/Bat Mitzvah.

As for your appearance, you don't want to bring all of your make-up and spend half of the evening in the ladies room reapplying. You might, if you have oily skin, want to buy some oil absorbing sheets. This packet will fit in the smallest of handbags, and you can get rid of the shine with a quick trip to the ladies room once or twice during the event. This should keep your skin looking great for pictures, and it won't smudge your make-up. As for hair, there's not much that you can do, once you've been styled and the spray has dried. Curls will gradually fall, but so will everybody else's so don't worry about it.

You will also need to pack along any decorations that you were unable to finish the previous day. Before the ceremony, try to finish that up, or have a friend help you with it. Place a seating chart somewhere visible if you plan to have one. It can be chaotic if there are only place cards in a huge room. Seating charts on poster board help people to find their seats more quickly. You may also want to contact your vendors (DJ, florist, magician, caterer, etc...) on the morning of the event, to ensure that all is progressing as planned and that everyone knows what their tasks are and where things are taking place.

One very important element not to forget on the Bar/Bat Mitzvah day is vendor fees. Although many require the full payment in advance, some such as most DJs will accept cash payments on the day of the event. If you plan to do this, there is an organized way to go about it. Divide the money into envelopes. Write the vendor's name on the outside of the envelope and seal his/her cash inside. This way, on the big day, you won't be fishing around your purse looking for bills. When you get to the venue, simply hand each vendor his/her envelope and your job is done.

Don't allow yourself to lose your head in all of the excitement of the day. On the same token, don't allow yourself to be burdened by unnecessary stress on this occasion either. With proper planning, you can accomplish all that you need to on this day without upsetting yourself into a frenzy.

Speeches

Preparing any speech can be very stressful and preparing a speech for such an big event as a Bar Mitzvah can be especially challenging. There are different affiliations you can build your speech on. Your speech can be conservative, orthodox, reformed, etc. The best way to prepare such a particular speech is to keep it conservative, as not to offend any guests.

Here are some basic guide lines one should include in a speech: Welcoming the guests. Greet the people who are attending your Bar Mitzvah warmly and make them feel comfortable. It is important to break the ice. This will help you, who is giving the speech, to feel more relaxed and the guests to feel more comfortable. Making jokes throughout the speech is an excellent way to keep the gesture lighthearted and interesting.

Include stories in your speech. Telling your guest a short story can help build the body of your speech and help you strengthen the point you want to make at the end. This is also a way of grabbing the guests attention and keeping everyone interested in what you are saying. A story can be anything from your own experience, an experience of another person to a story from the Torah.

Remember that the Bar Mitzvah is a celebration. Keep the speech lighthearted and of medium length. Write key words down on a small piece of paper to keep you on track, if you tend to wander off of what you are taking about, and keep them handy.

Talk about what this occasion means to you personally. Calibrating on how the event effects you and how you feel about the occasion is always a key part of a speech. It makes the speech more personal and touching. It gives the speech a warm feeling and not the feeling of a cold, impersonal piece you found on the Internet.

Family and friends. Mentioning family and friend in a speech and what they have done for you is a way you can pay tribute to them for always being there to support you.

Thank everyone who made the day possible. It is very important to thank the people who helped make the day possible. Thank them warmly and from the heart.

Prepare thoroughly. Preparing and knowing your speech by heart helps to build confidence. This also makes it easier to deliver the speech flawlessly.

End the speech strongly. Wrap up all the loose ends in your ending lines and try to make one last precise point before ending. Leave an impression and make an impact. Use an ending line which you guests will remember. You should always end your speech on a positive note and leave everyone smiling.

Last but not least, relax. If you are well prepared things will flow naturally. If you are not accustomed to speaking in front of a group of people, you can keep a piece of paper with you and use it as a backup if you forget any part of the speech.

Best wishes

One can often be at a loss for words at a occasion such as a Bar Mitzvah or Bat Mitzvah. If you say something true and from the heart one can never go wrong, but most of us have trouble translating our feelings into words. Here are a few examples of best wishes you can write on a card or give to the person who is celebrating their Bar Mitzvah or Bat Mitzvah. The examples shown can be edited to fit either a Bar Mitzvah or a Bat Mitzvah.

We are so very proud of you on this very special day. Congratulations on your Bar Mitzvah!

Mazel Tov! May you prosper and grow into a marvelous example of a Jewish woman, who's children will be proud to follow in her footsteps. Congratulations on your Bat Mitzvah!

Mazel Tov! May light radiate through you and may this be the most special time in your life. Congratulations on your Bar Mitzvah!

Congratulations on you Bar Mitzvah! May you go from strength to strength!

For you on you Bar Mitzvah: May light and wisdom always guide you ways. Congratulations!

Mazel Tov on your Bar Mitzvah! May your heart always be true. May success greet you on your path of life. We are so proud of you. Congratulations!

On this very special day: Your friends and family are so proud of you! Congratulations!

To a very special boy: Congratulations on your Bar Mitzvah!

Mazel Tov on your Bar Mitzvah! May your life be filled with happiness and riches.

Wishing you happiness and prosperity on your Bar Mitzvah. Mazel Tov!

A Bat Mitzvah remembrance: May you prosper in the teaching of the Torah. May longevity and beauty embrace your paths.

Mazel Tov! May blessings rain down upon you! Congratulations on your Bat Mitzvah!

Hope you enjoy is remarkable day! Be blessed! Congratulations on you Bat Mitzvah!

Mazel Tov! May you receive everything your heart desires! Congratulations on your Bar Mitzvah!

Congratulations on your becoming a Bar Mitzvah. May you flourish in your dreams. Best wishes.

May this wonderful occasion be a inspiration to you throughout your life. Mazel Tov!

Mazel Tov! May the wisdom of the Torah enrich and guide you! Congratulations on you Bar Mitzvah

Afterwards

After the balloons have deflated and the relatives returned home, you may think that the work is done. Well, not everything is done. You and your child both have some post-party responsibilities which require your attentions. As a parent, you need to tie up any loose ends; your child has another very important duty- thank you's.

Often times caterers, florists, and venues will require a deposit in addition to the fee. If you have paid anything on top of the fee, be sure to get your money back. You will also need to follow up with your photographer to ensure that he receives payment, and that you receive your prints. The photographer is usually the only person whose service you will still need after the occasion. Pay him in a timely manner, and be polite but professional with him. If he promised your photos by a certain date, hold him to it. If you never received a given date, then be patient. It takes time to touch up the photos, and you want him to do a good job. Wrap up any other issues that need taken care of on the business end of things. Once this is done, you can relax and start adding to your scrapbook all of the memories that you made that day.

Your child has the more important aftermath job to do. The bigger the party, the bigger the stack of gifts- this is true. However, the more gifts received, the more thank you's need to be written. Your child should begin crafting his/her thank you notes immediately after the event. Everyone should have received their notes within a month or so. Notes should be specific if the gift was not money. For example, "Thank you so much Mrs. So and so for the mp3 player, I can't wait to use it." For money gifts, it is better not to pinpoint the exact amount.

Instead of, "Thank you for the $100," say, "Thank you for your generous gift." He or she might even say, "I'm going to use it toward buying blank." If your child doesn't know what he/she is going to do with it, just keep it general. The fact that your child sent thank you notes will make people feel good.

Once thank you notes have been addressed, you will want to make sure that your child cashes or deposits any checks that he/she has received. If a person writes a check and it doesn't get deposited until a few months later, you could possibly be putting that person in an awkward financial situation.

After all of the post-party work is done, then you can relax and enjoy looking at pictures, and remembering all of the fun. Be sure not to forget to finish what you started though, and tie up all of your loose ends after the Bar/Bat Mitzvah. Once this is completed, you are officially free from all of the stress that came with this momentous occasion.

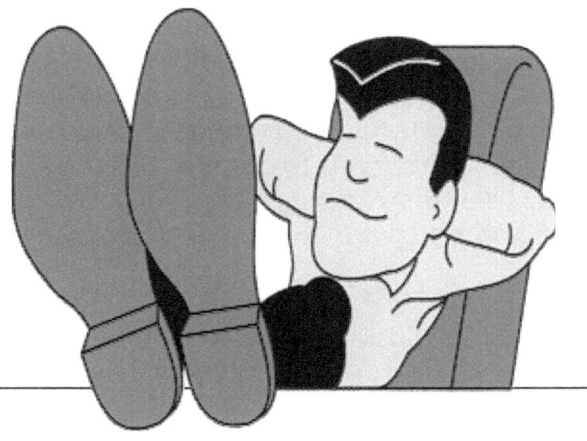

Preserving Memories

So when the checks have all been cashed, thank you's sent, and the unwanted gifts exchanged, what's left to do? Now it's time to preserve all of the memories that you made that day. The 4X6 photos that your friends and relatives sent you will surely be lost if left unattended. The portraits done by the photographer will fade in time. So how do you ensure that these memorable photos will last as long as possible?

Collect all of the photos from friends and create a scrapbook or album of candid photos. Chances are, your guests caught some funny moments which weren't captured by your professional photographer. So you'll definitely want to hang on to these pictures. Make a day of it with your child, and compile a scrapbook of these memories. It's a great way to spend time with your son or daughter and relive the memories.

As for your professional photographer, you should have him/her create a CD with all of the event pictures on it. Keep the disc in a safe location. In this manner, no matter what happens to the prints that you order, you will always have a digital record of the day. In addition to the CD, have some prints made to scrapbook or put in albums. Also, print some smaller ones to send to relatives who could not attend. Make a few 8X10s to frame and display in your home, so that you'll always be reminded of the wonderful celebration. Another great way to display pictures is to create a memory wall. Use a large multi-photo frame and place lots of 4X6's in it and hang it in your living room.

If you enjoy more high tech gadgetry, get yourself a digital photo frame. You can load your digital pictures into the frame, and it will scroll through them all, the same way that your computer does with a slide show.

Also, if you hired a videographer to document the ceremony and/or reception, be sure to get multiple DVDs. Whereas you are better off than the old VHS tapes that dry out, DVDs are prone to scratching. So make sure that one drop or scrape doesn't destroy the video, and get a few copies of it made.

Regardless of the method you used to capture memories, make certain that you hang onto them by storing them in a safe and organized fashion. Photos tossed into a cardboard box and left in the attic will not survive for very long. Treasure your prints and they will last for a lifetime. Store your digital media properly, and always keep a backup. If you are careful and organized, your Bar/Bat Mitzvah picture memories will last even when your own memory begins to fail. So take good care, and enjoy reliving this special day for years to come.

4 BONUS OFFERS!!

To receive the most up-to-date bonus offers —
Just simply **email me** at:

mitzvahtipsbook@getresponse. com

I hate spam as much as you do. I promise, your information will
not be shared or sold.

… Feel free to give me your feedback when you write to me, I
love to hear what you found most useful!

Enjoy!

Robert A. Starkey

Author

www.ingramcontent.com/pod-product-compliance
Lightning Source LLC
Chambersburg PA
CBHW021237280526
45784CB00005B/2123